MYSTERIOUS DISAPPEARANCES

John Townsend

Chicago, Illinois

Printed and bound in China
08
10 9 8 7 6 5 4 3 2

Library of Congress Cataloging-in-Publication Data
Townsend, John.
    Mysterious disappearances / John Townsend.
        p. cm. -- (Out there)
Summary: Relates cases of people who have mysteriously disappeared, never to be found.
Includes bibliographical references.
    ISBN 1-4109-0561-6 (lib. bdg.), 1-4109-0962-X (Pbk.)
    ISBN 978-1-4109-0561-1 (lib. bdg.), 978-1-4109-0962-6 (Pbk.)
    1. Disappearances (Parapsychology)--Juvenile literature. [1. Disappearances (Parapsychology) 2. Missing persons. 3. Curiosities and wonders.] I. Title. II. Series.
    BF1389.D57T69 2004
    001.94--dc21
                        2003010543

Acknowledgments
The publisher would like to thank the following for permission to reproduce photographs: p. 4 Sean Dempsey/PA Photos; pp. 5, 15 Photodisc; pp. 6–7 James A. Sugar/Corbis; p. 6 (left) Maiman Rick/Corbis; p. 7 (right) Aviation-Images.com/Mark Wagner; pp. 8–9 Getty Images Stone; p. 8 (left) Sinclair Stammers/Science Photo Library; pp. 9 (right), 30 (top), 42, 46–47, 49 (right) Corbis; pp. 17, 30 (bottom), 32 (right) Popperfoto; p. 10 (right) Bill Bachman; pp. 10 (left), 11, 21, 27, 28 (top), 28 (bottom), 29, 39 Bettmann/Corbis; p. 13 Hulton/Getty; pp. 14–15 Sue Anderson/Island Focus; p. 16 (left) J. Jackson/Robert Harding; p. 18 Bisson Bernard/Corbis; pp. 18–19 Worldsat International Inc./Science Photo Library; p. 19 Science Photo Library; p. 20 Ralph A. Clavenger/Corbis; p. 21 Kos Picture Source; p. 22, Dennis Degnan/Corbis; pp. 22–23 Naval Historical Foundation; p. 23 Aviation Images; p. 24 (left) J. Knighton & Worldsat International Inc./Science Photo Library; pp. 24–25 Jack Fields/Corbis; p. 25 Robert Harding; p. 26 M. Alexander/Robert Harding; p. 31 Rykoff Collection/Corbis; p. 32 (left) Eric and David Hosking/Corbis; p. 33 Nationwide News, Australia/Newspix; pp. 34 (left), 34–35, 47 John Cleare/Mountain Camera; p. 35 Bolante Anthony/Corbis; p. 36 (left) Fretwater Press; pp. 36–37, 48 Pat O'Hara/Corbis; p. 37 (right) Getty Images Taxi; p. 40 (left) Adam Woolfitt/Corbis; pp. 40–41Terry W. Eggers/Corbis; p. 41 Owaki-Kulla/Corbis; pp. 42–43 Brian A. Vikander/Corbis; p. 43, 44, 44–45 Associated Press; p. 45 Australian Associated Press; p. 46 Massimo Mastrorillo/Corbis; p. 49 (left) Ronald Grant Archive; p. 50 Chris Collins/Corbis; pp. 50–51 Anthony Blake Picture Library; p. 51 NHPA.
Cover photographer used with permission of Robert Harding Picture Library.

CONTENTS

Some words are shown in bold, **like this.** You can find out what they mean by looking in the glossary. You can also look for them in the "Weird Words" box at the bottom of each page.

WITHOUT A TRACE

PLAYING DEAD

Some people fake their own death or run away to escape from their past. They may want to fool:

- The police
- A gang
- An **assassin**
- The secret service
- The IRS (Internal Revenue Service)
- A nagging partner!

So they disappear forever . . .

In the time it takes you to read this page, someone will be reported missing. Hundreds of people around the world disappear every day.

Many will turn up somewhere soon. Others might be found after a long time. Some will never be seen again. They vanish from the face of the earth forever. Or so it seems.

> Dear Sue,
> I'm leaving you. Don't try to look for me. You'll never find me. I'm starting a new life in South America . . .

MISSING
HAVE YOU SEEN RICHARD?

Richard, age 24, was last seen in his office in Chicago at about 4 pm Friday, October 13. He is 6 feet, 1 inch tall of average build with short brown hair and a freckle on his left cheek. When last seen, he was wearing a blue-and-white striped shirt and black pants.

Anyone with information as to his whereabouts should contact the police.

WHERE?

Strange cases still confuse the experts. Where do "the missing" go? These mysteries have puzzled the world for years. What happens to "the lost"? Who are the **victims?**

> A missing person poster can sometimes help to find people. **❝❝**

WEIRD WORDS   assassin killer who is hired to murder an important person

WHY?

Most people who disappear have a reason.
It could be one of the following:

- Perhaps they run away to start new lives.
- Perhaps they are unwell, need help, or forget who they are.
- Perhaps they are taken by other people. Kidnappings do happen. Sometimes they end in murder.
- Perhaps they get lost, go the wrong way, fall, or get stuck. It may take a long time for a search party to find them.

Occasionally a whole group of people vanishes. No reasons or clues are left behind. Will we ever solve these mysteries of the disappeared?

> Sometimes people run away. But this cannot explain every mysterious disappearance. **》》**

FIND OUT LATER ...

Why will some mysteries never be solved?

Why do some places have a bad reputation?

Why did this person disappear?

victim person who gets hurt or killed

WHATEVER HAPPENED?

GONE IN A FLASH

In 1975 Jackson Wright drove with his wife to New York City through the Lincoln Tunnel. He stopped the car to wipe the windshield. When he got back inside, his wife was gone. He had heard nothing. Martha Wright had simply disappeared, never to be seen again.

Jackson Wright swore his wife disappeared outside the tunnel. Police found no signs of a struggle.

It seems strange that people can be here one minute and gone the next. Can they just disappear, never to be seen again? It happened to a man named Jerrold Potter in 1968.

OVER MISSOURI

A passenger airplane was flying from Kankakee, Illinois, to Dallas, Texas. It was a clear summer day. During the flight, Mrs. Potter saw her husband, Jerrold, make his way to the back of the plane to use the bathroom. She never saw him again.

After some time, she asked the staff to check if he was all right. When they looked, the bathroom was empty. He was nowhere on the plane.

WEIRD WORDS   cabin room for passengers or crew on an aircraft

OPEN DOOR

The rear door of the airplane was open slightly. This did not suck out the air from inside the plane, as it would in modern planes. That is because the **cabin** was not **pressurized** as it would be today. A chain for keeping the door shut was found on the floor.

Had Jerrold Potter bumped into the door and fallen out of the plane? To do this, he would have needed to turn a big door handle that was hard to move. No one saw or heard him fall.

So what did happen to Jerrold Potter? A long search was made along the airplane's flight path. His body was never found. The mystery remains to this day.

KEY QUESTIONS ABOUT JERROLD POTTER

- If he had fallen, would he have been able to push the door almost shut behind him?
- Did he think the exit was the bathroom door?
- Was he pushed?
- Did he jump on purpose?
- Was he ill or confused?

His wife said he was fine.

How could someone disappear from a flying airplane?

Could Jerrold have mistaken the exit door for the bathroom?

pressurized sealed space in which the air pressure is controlled

Everyone has a special DNA pattern.

FINDING THE MISSING

When the police find human remains, how can they **identify** them? Now the police can quickly match the details of a missing person with a dead body. **Databases** of dental records or **DNA** information can help solve many mysteries. This was not possible a few years ago.

MISSING IN THE NIGHT SKY

The man wore a suit and tie. He carried a briefcase and wore sunglasses. He said his name was Dan Cooper. He bought a ticket for a one-way flight from Portland, Oregon, to Seattle, Washington. It was November 1971.

What happened to the passenger named Dan Cooper is a great mystery. After the plane had taken off, he handed a note to the flight attendant. The note said that he had a bomb. He said the crew had to land at Seattle and pick up $200,000 and four parachutes. The crew followed his orders and the passengers got off, unaware of the **drama.** The plane took off once more with just the crew and Cooper on board.

database computer records for sorting information quickly
DNA genetic code in our cells

STORMY NIGHT

With the cash tied to his body and a parachute on his back, Cooper jumped from the plane over 2 miles (3 kilometers) up. The night outside was freezing. The wind chill made it 158 °F (70 °C) below zero. Could he **survive** in only a raincoat? Cooper and his parachute were never found. Did he die or did he get away with the money?

In 1980 a boy found $5,880 in decaying bills by the Columbia River, northwest of Vancouver. They matched those given to Cooper. Maybe he was killed in the jump, but no evidence has ever been found. And what happened to the rest of the cash? No one knows.

The Columbia River may hide the missing $194,120.

UNSOLVED MYSTERY

Did Cooper fall into the Columbia River? After his disappearance, he became something of a hero. A movie of his story came out ten years later. In 2000 a woman in Florida said her dying husband confessed to being Cooper. We will never know the truth now.

identify find out someone's name
survive to stay alive despite dangers

FOR THE RECORD

Harold Holt was the twenty-second prime minister of Australia. The **official** record said:

> Harold Holt—born in Sydney in 1908. Prime minister for less than two years. Died in Melbourne in 1967 (presumed drowned).

The mystery now seems to be forgotten.

MISSING IN THE OCEAN

The news stunned the world. Australia's prime minister was missing. Harold Holt vanished on December 17, 1967. He has never been found.

Harold Holt was a fit and healthy 59-year-old. He was a good swimmer. As always, he had run down the beach to begin his day with a swim. It all happened at Cheviot Beach where the huge waves crash onto the sand. Only strong swimmers can handle the waters there. Not many people were around and so no one saw what happened. Harold Holt was never seen again. Soon the quiet beach was full of police.

Harold Holt vanished on this beach in Australia.

official according to the rules and records
rumor story based on gossip

MASSIVE HUNT

The air, land, and sea search began that afternoon. It went on for days. No **trace** of the prime minister was ever found.

There were many **rumors** about the missing man. People said his job had been too hard for him. Perhaps he had planned his own disappearance. Maybe he wanted to get away from it all and start a new life. Others said he was a spy and a submarine had taken him away!

Perhaps he was not as fit as he thought he was. Did he drown? Did the waves crash him into rocks? Did a shark get him? It is unlikely now that the world will ever know.

ANOTHER FAMOUS MAN LOST AT SEA

Glenn Miller led popular dance bands during World War II. In 1944 he took off ahead of his band in a small plane from England to Paris. When the band arrived in Paris, they found no trace of Miller. Glenn Miller and his plane were never found.

The Glenn Miller band became even more famous when its leader disappeared.

trace sign, track, or footprint

11

INTO THIN AIR

One famous vanishing mystery is of the **deserted** ship called the *Mary Celeste*. The mystery has never been solved and probably never will be.

The ship set sail from New York in 1872. It had a crew of seven men. The American captain was named Benjamin Briggs. He had his wife and two-year-old daughter with him. The ship was heading for Genoa, Italy. It was carrying a **cargo** of alcohol across the Atlantic Ocean. A few days later, the ship was seen drifting near Portugal.

Sailors from another American sailing ship called the *Dei Gratia* climbed aboard the empty *Mary Celeste*. The ship's decks and sails were wet after recent storms. The lifeboat was missing.

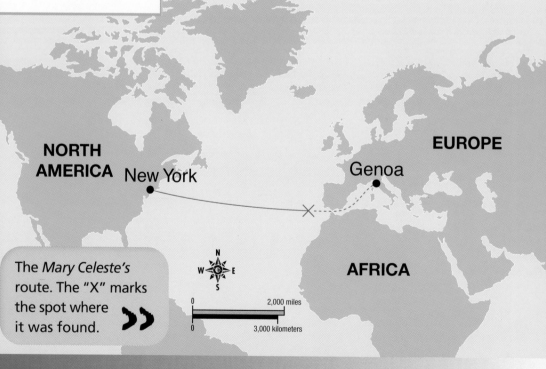

NORTH AMERICA New York

EUROPE

Genoa

AFRICA

The *Mary Celeste's* route. The "X" marks the spot where it was found. »

N
W ⊕ E
S

0 ———— 2,000 miles

0 ———— 3,000 kilometers

cargo goods carried on a ship or aircraft
deserted left empty

We will never know what happened to this ship.

WHY DID THEY LEAVE THE SHIP?

- Pirates? Nothing was stolen.
- Illness? Why would they *all* leave?
- Fighting? There was no blood or signs of **violence**.
- Bad weather? They would have been safer staying on the ship.
- Dangerous cargo? Everything was safe and sound.

NO CLUES

There was no sign of a struggle on board the *Mary Celeste*. Yet the ten people who had been on the ship had vanished. They were never seen again. Captain Briggs was a good sailor with a lot of experience. Why would he order everyone to leave the ship? Nothing in the **ship's log** gave any clues. So what made them leave in a hurry?

For years people have asked what happened to the ship's passengers and the missing lifeboat. Did it sink? Did they land on an island and die of thirst? Did a storm kill them? The truth is, we will never know.

New York, Nov. 3, 1872
My dear Mother:
It seems real homelike since Sarah and Sophia got here, and we enjoy our little quarters . . . Our vessel is in beautiful trim and I hope we shall have a fine passage but I have never been in her before and can't say how she'll sail.
Hoping to be with you in the spring with much love.
I am yours affectionately,
Benj

An extract from Captain Briggs's last letter, written on board the *Mary Celeste*.

hold space in the lower part of a ship for storing the cargo
ship's log diary written up each day by the captain

AT THE EDGE OF THE HEBRIDES

Of all the Scottish islands, Eilean Mor is the most mysterious. It was said to be haunted by the dead sailors lost in its dangerous waters. The lighthouse is 15 miles (24 kilometers) west of the Isle of Lewis. It still flashes every 30 seconds.

Eilean Mor is quiet but mysterious.

THE ISLAND OF THE DEAD

The small Scottish island of Eilean Mor had a new lighthouse. Three men lived and worked in the lighthouse to warn ships away from rocks. Lighthouses were not **automatic** then.

On December 26, 1900, the supply boat visited the island, as it did every two weeks. It brought food and picked up one of the lighthouse keepers for his break. This time there was something wrong. The new 82-foot- (25-meter-) high lighthouse was deathly quiet. There was no sign of life on the small island. There was no flag and no empty boxes on the **jetty.**

The landing party entered the **deserted** lighthouse. The clock had stopped, the fire was out, and the three men who should have been on duty were missing.

jetty small pier or platform that juts into water for the anchoring of boats

GHOSTLY IN THE COLD SUNLIGHT

There were no signs of **violence** in the lighthouse. The main room was clean and neat. There was food in the cupboards and everything was as it should have been.

There were no raincoats hanging up. That was odd, because all three men would not normally go outside at the same time.

A bad storm had struck two weeks before. The log for December 12 said:

Waves very high. Tearing at lighthouse. Storm still raging, cannot go out.

The last entry in the log was three days later on December 15:

1 P.M. Storm ended, sea calm.

That was the last that was heard of the three lighthouse keepers.

WHERE DID THEY GO?

Some said the men had been turned into crows by an ancient **curse.** Others told tales of skeleton pirates carrying them away. UFOs are reported in this part of the world. Did aliens carry off the men? Or were all three men washed away by a giant wave?

violence act that uses dangerous force

HUNTING FOR CLUES

If the *Waratah* sank, nobody can guess where. Searches with submarines have tried to find it. In 1999 a team found a wreck. The world waited for news and the report came: "The wreck is not, repeat not the *Waratah*." Maybe one day the *Waratah* will be found.

Divers can find it difficult to identify a wreck underwater.

WHAT HAPPENED TO THE *WARATAH*?

The great new **steamship** the *Waratah* was said to be unsinkable. But one of the big mysteries of the sea is "Where did the *Waratah* go?" No one knows why it disappeared. Even after many searches, the ship has never been found.

On its return **maiden voyage** from Sydney, Australia, to London, England, the ship vanished. It disappeared somewhere in the Indian Ocean off the coast of South Africa. It left the port of Durban in South Africa on July 26, 1909. On board were 119 crew and the 92 passengers who had not stayed in Australia. It was unlucky for these passengers that they did not stay, since something terrible happened. To this day, nobody knows what.

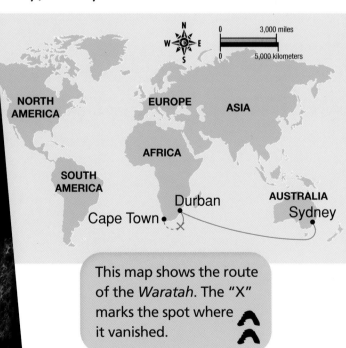

This map shows the route of the *Waratah*. The "X" marks the spot where it vanished.

gale storm with very high winds
maiden voyage first journey

WARNING

Claude Sawyer was a passenger on the *Waratah*. The ship was comfortable, and the three-month journey was passing without any problems. But one night Claude had a bad dream. Just before the ship arrived at Durban, he felt something awful was about to happen. He sensed that the ship was **unstable,** so he got off at Durban and sent a message to his wife in London:

THOUGHT *WARATAH* TOP-HEAVY. LANDED IN DURBAN.

No one listened to his warning. The great ship sailed on without him. He watched the last thin trail of smoke . . . and it vanished from sight forever.

THE OFFICIAL RECORD

Reports said the *Waratah* must have sunk in a bad **gale.** There were other ideas as well. Had it been sucked down by a huge **whirlpool?** There were stories about shipwrecked children, life jackets washed up in Australia, and messages in bottles. Are any of these stories true?

A painting of the *Waratah.*

unstable not steady, unsafe
whirlpool powerful circular current in the ocean

THE BERMUDA TRIANGLE

The ocean has more than its share of "missing mysteries." Hundreds of people vanish at sea each year. One area is known for swallowing ships, planes, and people up. The Bermuda Triangle sends a shiver down the spines of many sailors and pilots.

BERMUDA TRIANGLE FACT SHEET

This is an area off the southeastern Atlantic coast of the United States. It is famous because many ships, small boats, and aircraft have gotten lost here. "There is a popular belief that **supernatural** powers are at work. This is **science fiction.**" U.S. Coastguard

A TERRIFYING RECORD

The sea between Florida, Bermuda, and Cuba holds strange secrets. In the past 100 years, more than 20 planes and 50 ships have been lost in the Bermuda Triangle. Nothing has been found of them, or of about a thousand people who have disappeared. Other parts of the world's oceans also seem to have more than their share of disappearances. These areas are sometimes called Devil's Triangles.

More than 50 ships have vanished in the Bermuda Triangle. **‹‹**

air traffic control people and equipment that direct aircraft

ONLY NATURAL

The Bermuda Triangle may be a **myth.** Some people say the disappearances are just accidents. They say they are caused by bad sailors who do not know the area. The calm waters around Bermuda might fool them. These are some of the world's busiest shipping lanes, so there are bound to be a few losses. But why do planes disappear as well? Why is wreckage rarely found?

MISSING FOR TEN MINUTES

Perhaps time gets lost in the Bermuda Triangle. A Boeing 727 once disappeared from radar screens and **air traffic control** feared the worst. Thankfully, the plane landed safely ten minutes later. The crew had flown through fog. All their watches were ten minutes slow. Why?

GETTING LOST

Maybe ships can get sucked into whirlpools. But what happens to the planes?

The Gulf Stream is a strong ocean current off the east coast of the United States. Around Bermuda it may drag boats hundreds of miles off course. The unusual **magnetism** in this area might make matters worse. Add some fog, a giant wave, or a **whirlpool,** and who knows?

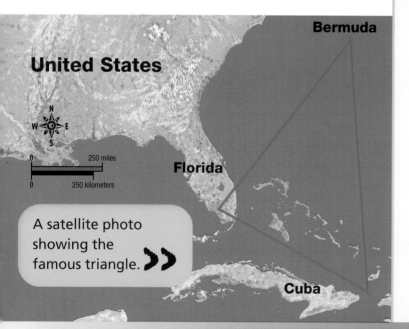

Bermuda

United States

N
W—E
S

0   250 miles
0   350 kilometers

Florida

A satellite photo showing the famous triangle. >>

Cuba

magnetism force that makes a ship's compass point north
supernatural forces beyond the laws of nature

19

INSIDE THE BERMUDA TRIANGLE IN 1881

The *Ellen Austin* was sailing from London to New York when its crew saw a drifting ship. Six of them went aboard and sailed in the empty ship as fog fell around them. The next day, the mystery ship was gone. So were the six men. They were never seen again.

NEVER SEEN AGAIN

One of the most famous mysteries of the Bermuda Triangle occurred in 1963. A huge **tanker,** the *Sulphur Queen*, simply vanished along with its 39 crew members.

Two weeks before its last voyage, inspectors checked the *Sulphur Queen* for safety. The ship was in very good shape. There were new life jackets and all the lifeboats had been repaired. All its radios were in full working order. Everything was ready to go. Yet the ship disappeared without warning in the Bermuda Triangle. It failed to arrive in port. On February 7, the Coastguard was told that the *Sulphur Queen* was missing.

Just a year later, in 1964, the term "Bermuda Triangle" was used for the first time.

When the *Sulphur Queen* vanished, some debris was left floating in the water.

debris scattered remains
SOS signal for help. Is is short for "Save Our Ship."

HOPELESS SEARCH

Rescue teams searched 350,000 square miles (906,500 square kilometers) of ocean and failed to find any clues. What had happened to the *Sulphur Queen*? How can you lose a huge tanker? Why had there been no **SOS** signal?

Days later a foghorn was seen floating in the water. Then a ship's name board with "*Marine Sulphur Queen*" written on it was picked up. A few torn life jackets looked as if sharks had attacked them.

Had the **sulfur** on board the ship exploded? Experts tested the **debris** and there was no sign of fire or sulfur. It still remains one of the Bermuda Triangle's deepest mysteries.

CARRIED BY CURRENTS

In 1991 Michael Plant took off in his small powerboat, *Coyote*. Near Bermuda, he reported something odd. He kept losing electrical power and his long-range radio was not working. No more was heard from him. Months later, his boat was found upside down and miles away. Michael was never found.

The Coastguard examines the torn life jackets and fog horn—all that was left of the *Sulphur Queen*.

sulfur   yellow mineral used to make gunpowder
tanker   huge ship for carrying liquid materials

WHERE IS FLIGHT 19?

In 1991 five crashed planes were found in 656 feet (200 meters) of water off the coast of Florida. Divers later proved that these were not from Flight 19. The final resting place of the planes and their crews is still the Bermuda Triangle's secret.

THE DISAPPEARANCE OF FLIGHT 19

The story of 27 men and 6 planes that disappeared in the Bermuda Triangle has puzzled the world for years. How and why they vanished one day at the end of 1945 is a mystery. Was it the **curse** of the Bermuda Triangle or just human error?

STUDENT PILOTS

On December 5, 1945, five bombers flew from the Fort Lauderdale Naval Air Station in Florida on a training flight over the water. Charles Taylor was the pilot in charge of thirteen students. He was in constant radio contact with all his fellow pilots. Over an hour into the flight, Taylor said his compass was not working. He was not sure where the student pilots were.

The beauty of the Bermuda area hides its dangers.

fate events that a person has no control over

FROM BAD TO WORSE

The weather grew worse. It was hard to see and the pilots were lost. They began to argue about which way to go. Taylor said he was right and they should fly east. Their planes were running out of fuel, the sea was getting rough, and darkness was falling. They still had no idea where they were.

SILENCE

The last signal from Flight 19 was heard at 7:04 P.M. After that, the radios went dead. Planes searched the area all that night and the next day. There was no sign of the five missing planes. The **fate** of the fourteen men was never explained.

THE OTHER MYSTERY LOSS

To make matters worse, one of the rescue planes also disappeared hours later. It had thirteen men on board and there was no signal for help. It simply vanished. A report said that one of the crew had been smoking—which may have blown up the aircraft.

Perhaps the bombers exploded. But there were no signs of **debris** in the ocean.

MORE DEVIL'S TRIANGLES

TRIANGLE OF DANGER

On the other side of the world from the Bermuda Triangle is another mysterious area of ocean. Danger seems to **lurk** in the Dragon's Triangle. It is in the Pacific Ocean between Japan, Taiwan, and the island of Guam. Many ships and planes have disappeared there.

THE DRAGON'S TRIANGLE

The Dragon's Triangle between Japan, Taiwan, and Guam is another strange area of ocean. It is on the **Ring of Fire,** where earthquakes strike. **Seaquakes** can cause giant waves. If a **volcano** erupts, or explodes, under the ocean, the waves will bubble and steam.

Islands have formed overnight in the Dragon's Triangle when **lava** has shot up from the **seabed**. Old maps show islands that no longer exist because earthquakes destroyed them.

The seabed here drops down miles to the deepest ocean **trenches** in the world. This can make strong currents and **whirlpools.** Sudden fogs and powerful storms are common. It is not the safest place to sail a small boat!

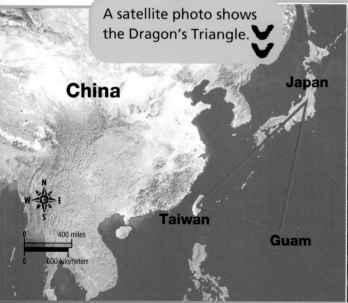

A satellite photo shows the Dragon's Triangle.

China

Japan

Taiwan

Guam

N
W E
S

0   400 miles

0   600 kilometers

lava hot, melted rock that comes out of volcanoes
lurk wait around, ready to strike

THE DRAGON ATTACKS

Like the Bermuda Triangle, this area has strange **magnetic** powers. A ship's compass can often fail and sailors get lost in the Dragon's Triangle. For over a thousand years, the Japanese have told of mysterious disappearances. Old tales tell of restless dragons coming up from the ocean to drag sailors down to underwater caves.

Yet it was not until the 1960s that the world began to take notice of the Dragon's Triangle. The news of lost boats began to make people wonder what was going on.

A huge Norwegian **tanker** vanished in 1975. The *Berge Istra* sank in minutes after the radio officer reported that the weather was fine. No **trace** of the ship was ever found.

LOST SUBMARINES

Between 1968 and 1986, thirteen Russian submarines were lost in the Dragon's Triangle. Hundreds of men died over a period of eighteen years.

What happened? The reasons were not always known. Sometimes it was fire or explosions. Other times, there seemed to be no reason why they disappeared.

There are many old **myths** about the Dragon's Triangle.

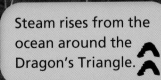

Steam rises from the ocean around the Dragon's Triangle.

seabed ocean floor; the bottom of the sea
seaquake earthquake under the ocean

THE *PATANELA*

A large yacht and its crew of four disappeared off the coast of Australia in 1988. Its **skipper** was skillful and the equipment on board was the very latest. The police thought another boat had hit the *Patanela*— yet no **debris** was ever found.

BASS STRAIT TRIANGLE

For years sailors have told of strange things in the stretch of ocean between Australia and Tasmania. Many people think of the Bass Strait as Australia's Bermuda Triangle. More ships and planes have vanished here than along the rest of the Australian coast. Maybe it is due to the strong **tides.** It could be the **gales** or the shifting **seabed.** Or is it just because of worn-out ships and bad sailors? Some sailors say there are more **sinister** powers at work in the water here.

The *Glasgow Citizen* was a ship full of gold miners. It left Melbourne, Australia in 1862 for New Zealand, but it disappeared forever in the Bass Strait.

Mysteries **lurk** off of Australia's coast.

This map shows the position of the Bass Strait.

Darwin

N
W E
S

0 — 400 miles

0 — 600 kilometers

Australia

Brisbane

Adelaide
Sydney
Canberra
Melbourne
Portland
Bass Strait

Tasmania
Hobart

sinister harmful or evil
skipper person in charge of a boat

THE VANISHING PILOT

Frederick Valentich was a 20-year-old pilot. One evening in 1978 he flew a small plane into the sky out over the Bass Strait. Suddenly radio contact began to fail. It sounded as if the engine was **stalling.** Frederick shouted his very last words into the radio at 7:12 P.M. on October 21: "An unknown aircraft is hovering on top of me." Then the radio went dead. Frederick and the plane were never found.

Another small aircraft disappeared nearby in the same year. People spoke of **UFOs** and strange lights. The mysteries are still unsolved.

SIX MINUTES BEFORE THE RADIO WENT DEAD...

19:06 hours

Valentich: Melbourne, is there any known traffic below five thousand feet?

Melbourne: No known traffic.

Valentich: There seems to be a large aircraft below five thousand.

Melbourne: What type of aircraft is it?

Valentich: It's four bright . . . it seems to me like landing lights . . .

What happened to the small plane that vanished in the Bass Strait?

stalling coming to a stop
tide daily rise and fall of the ocean

27

KIDNAP OR MURDER?

PANCHO VILLA

Ambrose Bierce was a famous American writer. He was known all over the country for his novels and work in newspapers. He set off for Mexico in 1913, when he was 71. Some people said he went to meet a Mexican **rebel** named Pancho Villa who was known to be **violent.** Nobody really knows what happened, but Ambrose Bierce was never seen again.

There were many stories. Some thought he died in the Grand Canyon. Others said he was shot by Pancho Villa or killed in a battle. Maybe he just lived to be a very old man in secret! We are unlikely to find the truth now.

Pancho Villa and his gang may have shot Ambrose Bierce.

Pancho Villa was a hero to some and a criminal to others. He and his gang were outlaws who killed Mexican soldiers. They were said to help the poor and steal cattle to sell. Pancho Villa was killed in 1923.

Ambrose Bierce before he disappeared.

lifestyle way people live and spend their free time
rebel fighter against the government

THE FAMOUS JUDGE

At one time Judge Crater was a very popular man in New York City. He was good at his job. He was also rich. His exciting **lifestyle** made him something of a star in the city. The 41-year-old lawyer loved yachts, fast cars, and beautiful women. But on the evening of August 6, 1930, he disappeared. One minute he was laughing with friends outside a restaurant. Then he got into a cab and was never seen again.

The biggest manhunt in New York history followed his disappearance. The search lasted for years and cost millions of dollars. But the mystery of Judge Crater still remains unsolved.

WHAT THE PAPERS SAID ABOUT JUDGE CRATER

KIDNAPPED AND MURDERED!

Judge was involved in crime

Crater lost his memory

he ran away with a secret girlfriend and his missing bank box . . .

After nine years, Judge Crater was declared dead. But reports that he was still alive appeared up to 60 years later.

Lucky Blackiet led the search for Judge Crater. Here he holds a picture of the missing man. **◄◄**

violent angry and dangerous

One of the last photos of the czar and his family. ∧∧

THE RUSSIAN ROYALS

The missing remains of the Russian royal family were thought to be hidden down a well. In 1991 some skeletons were dug up and their **DNA** was tested. At last this proved the bones belonged to the royal family. However, the bones of Alexei and Anastasia were not there.

RUSSIAN MYSTERY

The story of the Russian royal family was a **tragic** one. It was also full of mystery. Their disappearance was one of the secrets of the 1900s.

Nicholas was like a king, but was called a **czar.** He ruled all of Russia. He and his wife, Alexandra, had four girls and one boy. The youngest girl was Anastasia. Her younger brother, Alexei, was born in 1904. By 1914 Russia was fighting in World War I. Millions were killed in the war, and Russia was in bad shape. Some people blamed Czar Nicholas for being a bad leader. They started to plot against him.

This palace room is where the Russian royal family was murdered. ⌄⌄

czar emperor of Russia
house arrest being kept prisoner in an ordinary house

THE REVOLUTION

The Russian people had no food. While they starved, the royal family went on living in their beautiful palace. Workers began to take action. So did the army. In 1917 soldiers threw out the royal family and sent them to Siberia. They were under **house arrest** for 78 days. On the night of July 18, 1918, the royal family was told to go into the cellar with their servants and pets.

Armed men burst in and gunshots were fired. The rest was a mystery. Was the whole family killed? For many years no one knew what happened to their bodies. People still wonder what happened to Anastasia and Alexei.

ANASTASIA

Perhaps Anastasia **survived** the bullets because they bounced off diamonds in her clothes. She may have escaped.

Years later a woman named Anna Anderson said she was Anastasia. People were not sure. She married an American and died in 1984 at the age of 83.

Anastasia's story was the biggest mystery of all. ❮❮

---

tragic sad and terrible, with an unhappy ending

THE DINGO— WILD DOG OF AUSTRALIA

AUSTRALIAN MYSTERY

Lindy and Michael Chamberlain were camping in Central Australia. Two of their children were asleep in the tent. Their daughter Azaria was just ten weeks old. It was August 1980. Lindy looked up into the night sky from the barbecue where she was cooking. It was then she thought she heard a cry. Lindy thought it was the baby in the tent. She decided to go and check on her.

Dingoes have been known to attack animals as large as kangaroos.

A dingo is the size of a large dog. They sometimes hunt in packs. Dingoes rarely attack people, but some have killed children. Dingoes are now rare in most areas of Australia.

Lindy and Michael Chamberlain leaving Alice Springs court after Lindy was charged with murder.

arrest to capture and hold someone for questioning

TERROR

When Lindy got to the tent, she saw a large dingo coming out. It seemed to be dragging something along. She could not see what it was at first. Then the full horror hit her.

WORLD NEWS

Lindy ran into the tent to find Azaria missing. She screamed into the night, "A dingo took my baby!"

A search found nothing. Azaria was never seen again. The story hit the news and **rumors** began to spread. Nobody believed a dingo would steal a baby. There was something odd about this whole story.

The police had doubts, too. They began to think that Lindy had killed her own baby. She was **arrested** and charged. The trial made world news and Lindy was found guilty. Years later she was set free because of people's doubts. The world will never be sure what really happened to baby Azaria.

THE TRIAL

In October 1982 Lindy Chamberlain was sent to prison for killing her baby. Many people thought it was not fair because there was no proof. After a six-year fight, Lindy was set free. Who or what took Azaria remains a real mystery.

The Chamberlains' tent, in front of Ayer's Rock, where baby Azaria disappeared. ❯❯

ACCIDENT OR MORE?

GEORGE LEIGH MALLORY

Mallory was the only climber to take part in all three of the British climbs of Everest in the 1920s. He was born in 1886 and disappeared just before he turned 38. He was married with three small children. His family never knew what really happened to him.

At 29,000 feet (8,848 meters), Mount Everest is the highest point on the earth. Every climber dreamed of standing on its **summit,** until Edmund Hillary and Tenzing Norgay did so in 1953. They were the first men to get there—perhaps. That was part of the mountain's mystery for many years.

EVEREST MYSTERY

In 1924 George Mallory and Andrew Irvine tried to climb Everest. A climber far below spotted them when they were almost 1,000 feet (300 meters) from the top. Then heavy clouds came down. The two climbers vanished from sight. They never returned. Irvine's ice ax was found later. But the question was, were they the first to reach the top before they disappeared?

We will never know if Mallory reached the top of Everest.

WEIRD WORDS   **summit** very top of a mountain

75 YEARS LATER

For years, people could only guess what happened to the two climbers. Did they fall or freeze to death? Would they ever be found? Many climbers have been lost in terrible snowstorms on this cruel mountain.

Some answers came in May 1999. A party of climbers found a body about 2,000 feet (600 meters) from the top. They thought it must have been Mallory, and they gave him a proper burial. **DNA** tests later proved the body was Mallory. However, the mystery of his last hours still remained. Did he ever reach the top? Was he going up the mountain or coming down? Irvine has never been found. Everest still holds these secrets.

CLIMBING EVEREST

Thirty years after Mallory and Irvine disappeared on Everest, Edmund Hillary and Tenzing Norgay stood on its summit. Since then, many other climbers have reached the top. Mallory's grandson, George Mallory II, reached Mount Everest's summit in 1995.

These snow goggles were found in Mallory's pocket when his body was recovered in 1999.

STORIES

Many tales spread about Glen and Bessie Hyde:

- Did they have a fight and leave each other to start new lives?
- Did they find the trip too difficult and give up secretly?
- Did they fall in the river to be swept away forever?

GRAND CANYON MYSTERY

When a couple disappeared on their honeymoon in the Grand Canyon, a massive search was launched. The Grand Canyon in Arizona is a steep **gorge.** It is more than 200 miles (300 kilometers) long and more than half a mile deep. The truth has never been revealed about this couple, Glen and Bessie Hyde. It probably never will.

MISSING NEWLYWEDS

Glen and Bessie got married in November 1928. As a special honeymoon, they went **white-water rafting.** The Colorado River roars down the Grand Canyon. This would have been a real **challenge** for their home-made boat. Bessie Hyde wanted them to go down in history as the first couple to ride the **rapids** right through the Grand Canyon.

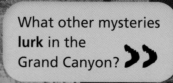

What other mysteries **lurk** in the Grand Canyon? »

WEIRD WORDS

destination place where a journey ends
gorge deep, rocky ravine carved by a river

NO SIGN

It seems that they almost made it. A month later, their boat was found floating in calm water. Inside it were a diary, a gun, clothes, and boots. The boat was just 46 miles (75 kilometers) from their **destination.** It seemed they did not make it as the first couple to ride the length of the Grand Canyon. The Hydes had just vanished. No **trace** of them was ever found. It was feared they had both drowned. The tale of the Hydes became a popular ghost story among river guides on the canyon. Their story was another mystery of the missing.

THE STRANGER

An old woman joined a Grand Canyon tour in 1971. She claimed to be Bessie Hyde. She said she had killed her husband before hiking off in 1928. A skeleton with a bullet in the skull was found in the canyon, but it was not Glen. The old woman was never seen again.

white-water rafting riding down a fast-flowing river in an inflatable boat, a canoe, or a kayak

1937

Amelia in 1937

PACIFIC OCEAN MYSTERY

The name Amelia Earhart was famous all around the world. She was born in Kansas in 1897. By the 1930s, she was a star. She was famous for flying airplanes. Amelia was a gifted pilot who showed that it was not just men who could fly alone. Everyone wanted to meet her.

WORLD FAMOUS

Amelia wrote books about her travels and set many flight records. In 1932 she was the first woman to fly alone across the Atlantic Ocean. That was amazing in the early days of aircraft. Then in 1935 she flew across the Pacific Ocean. Such a long flight was unheard of before then.

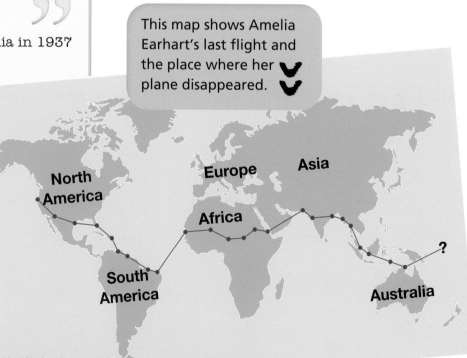

This map shows Amelia Earhart's last flight and the place where her plane disappeared.

equator imaginary line running east to west around the middle of the earth

ATTEMPT TO FLY AROUND THE WORLD

Amelia did not stop there. She wanted to be the first woman to fly all around the world, along the **equator.** Such a long flight was a dangerous **challenge.** Everyone thought she was very brave.

Amelia and her **navigator,** Fred Noonan, set off on their daring journey. While Amelia flew her Electra plane, Fred sat in the back with the maps. They covered thousands of miles. They were flying over the Pacific Ocean in the early hours of July 3, 1937, when they lost radio contact. It was near the Dragon's Triangle (see page 24). They and their plane were never found.

RUMORS

People even wondered if Amelia Earhart:

- was on a spy mission and was caught;
- was held by the Japanese during World War II;
- ran away with Fred, her navigator; or
- lived for years on an island in the South Pacific.

Amelia's Lockheed Electra plane just before take off on her last flight. Amelia and Fred are on board. ∨∨

navigator guide who plans the journey and decides which way to go

LOST AND FOUND

MISSING IN ROMANIA

In 1998 twelve-year-old Valentin disappeared in Romania. His parents called the police. A boy had just drowned in the Danube River. Valentin's parents **identified** him and held the funeral. Weeks later, Valentin came back—he had been staying with his aunt. No one knows who they had buried instead!

When people disappear for no reason, there is nothing their families can do but worry. If a person leaves without telling anyone, family and friends can only wait and hope.

BACK FROM THE DEAD

John Johnson was 69 when he went into the woods to get some logs in 1998. The woods stretched from his home in North Dakota into Canada. He walked too far and got lost in the miles of wild forest. He just could not find his way out again. Eight days later he stumbled onto a road. His family could not believe he was still alive.

John Johnson had eaten lily pads in the forest to survive.

The Danube River produced a new mystery.

character person's nature or personality

A NARROW ESCAPE

In May 2001 a student climbed down an old mine in Britain. He fell and pulled the rope down with him. There was no way he could climb out again.

For eleven long days he had to lie in the dark and cold. His family did not know where he was. He was miles from anywhere and it seemed hopeless. Then, by chance, some children came bird-watching. He called out when he heard them. They ran to get help. It took three hours to get him out of the mine. He went to the hospital and was soon back on his feet. Mystery solved!

MISSING IN UTAH

Aron Ralston was missing for five days in May 2003. He had gone hiking alone in Utah when a boulder fell and trapped his arm. He could not get away. It took him hours to cut off his arm using a knife. He escaped, got to a hospital, and **survived**!

BACK FROM THE FOREST

Even people who have been missing for years may still turn up one day. There is always hope.

MISSING, PRESUMED DEAD

At the end of World War II in 1945, American forces took over the island of Guam from the Japanese. The island is in the middle of the Pacific Ocean, in the Dragon's Triangle (see page 24). Japanese soldiers had to **surrender** to the U.S. Army. But some soldiers ran into the jungle to hide.

On January 24, 1972, two hunters found Shoichi Yokoi still hiding in the jungle. He had been missing for 28 years. He thought the war was still going on. His family had no idea he was still alive.

SHOICHI YOKOI

Shoichi worked as a tailor before World War II. While he was in the jungle, he made clothes from plant **fibers**. He ate coconuts, fruit, snails, eels, and rats. After he was found in 1972, he got married and went back to Guam for his honeymoon! He died in 1997 at the age of 82.

It is easy to hide in thick tropical jungle. Or get lost in it . . . .

fibers threads that can be made into cloth
surrender give up

ALONE IN THE JUNGLE

The famous story from 1971 of Juliane Koepcke is hard to believe. Everyone thought she was killed when a plane flying from Lima to Cuzco in Peru crashed in the Amazon jungle. The search party found that 91 passengers were killed. No one knew that Juliane had gotten out alive and was walking through the jungle.

Juliane was seventeen years old and was totally lost. She followed a stream. At last the stream led to a river. After walking for ten days, she found some people who saved her. The mystery is how Juliane **survived** both the crash and ten days alone in the jungle.

SEARCHING FOR THE LOST BACKPACKER

Louise Saunders was nineteen. In 2002, wearing just a T-shirt, shorts, and sneakers, she disappeared on Mount Tyson in Australia. She was lost in thick forest for three days. Louise finally found her way out. The mystery of her whereabouts was over!

Search and rescue teams cannot see into deep forests.

NEWS FLASH!

March 12, 2003
Kidnapped girl Elizabeth Smart has been found living just 15 miles (24 kilometers) from her home. Police were called when a woman saw three strange people carrying blankets in the streets of Sandy, Utah. Elizabeth was being held by a **drifter** couple, who have now been **arrested.** They used a wig to hide her blonde hair.

BACK IN THE NEWS

Two news stories in 2003 told of different fourteen-year-old girls who had disappeared. Their families could only wait and hope.

KIDNAPPING MYSTERY

A gunman kidnapped Elizabeth Smart in the early morning of June 5, 2002. He broke into her Salt Lake City, Utah, home and took her from the bedroom she shared with her younger sister. Hundreds of people helped to search streets and hills while police followed hundreds of **leads** until the trail went cold. The news story gripped the nation. Many people feared Elizabeth would never be found alive.

Nine months later, the police got a call. They rushed to the scene and found Elizabeth safe and well at last.

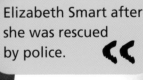

Elizabeth Smart after she was rescued by police. **〈〈**

anonymous from an unknown person
drifter someone with no real home or fixed address

MURDER VICTIM FOUND ALIVE

A teenage Australian girl was feared dead after being missing for nearly five years. Natasha Ryan was last seen in 1998 when she was taken away by an unknown man. The fourteen-year-old Natasha was returned to her shocked family after being found in a house nearby in April 2003. A man was already on trial for her murder. Natasha was found with the boyfriend she ran away with in 1998. Police searched a house and found her hiding in a cupboard. She could hardly see, since her eyes were not used to the light. She had hardly left the house in four years.

Found after five years

Neighbors next to the house where the missing girl was found said they did not even know a woman was living there. The first hint that eighteen-year-old Natasha was alive came in an **anonymous** note to the police.

Posters helped to spread the news of Elizabeth's kidnapping. ❱❱

Natasha Ryan spent five years in hiding. ❱❱

QUITE A HIKE

In 1986 a family moved from Wisconsin to Arizona. They took their cat, Sam. The next year they had to move back. Not wanting to uproot Sam again, they left him behind with friends. Guess what? Four years later Sam walked into the Wisconsin house— 1,400 miles (2,250 kilometers) away!

BACK FROM NOWHERE

Missing pets can be a real mystery. It is not just where they go that is a puzzle. How do they manage to come back when it seems **impossible?**

MISSING CAT

The Hicks family from Australia had a pet cat named Howie. In 1977, before going off on vacation, they went to leave Howie with some relatives who lived many miles away. While they were away, Howie disappeared. Everyone feared he had been stolen or killed. A year later, Howie turned up back at the Hicks' own home. He had crossed over 1,000 miles (1,600 kilometers) of Australian desert and wilderness to get there!

It seems impossible that a pet cat could cross the Australian desert . . .

MISSING DOGS

Dogs have a habit of disappearing, too. Some leave never to be seen again. They may run away to live in the wild, move in with someone else up the road, or get trapped somewhere.

TRAVELING DOG

In 1979 a German Shpherd named Nick was stolen when he was on vacation with his owner in Arizona. Somehow Nick escaped and headed home. But home was 2,000 miles (3,200 kilometers) away. He had to cross a desert, rivers, the Grand Canyon, and the 13,125-foot- (4,000-meter-) high mountains of Nevada. Four months later he appeared back home in Oregon. That's some dog!

. . . or that a pet dog could cross a mountain range.

CROSSING THE ROCKIES IN WINTER

In 1923 a collie named Bobbie got lost when his owners were on vacation in Indiana. He was 3,000 miles (4,800 kilometers) from home. Yet six months later he arrived back home in Oregon! He had crossed rivers and mountains. He was very tired and a little thin—but still very much alive!

FACT OR FICTION?

HOW DO YOU EXPLAIN IT?

A few months after David Lang's strange disappearance, his children found a mark in the field. The grass on the spot where their father vanished had turned yellow. It was a circle about 16 feet (5 meters) across. Very strange!

Flattened grass was the only sign left by David Lang's disappearance.

History is full of tales of people who just vanish from the face of the earth. Are these **legends,** fact, or pure fiction? There could be so many explanations.

NO ANSWER

There is a famous story that happened in September 1880 at a farm near Gallatin, Tennesee. David Lang was walking across a field when he turned to wave to a friend. A few seconds later, in full view of his wife, children, and friend, David Lang disappeared in midstep. They all ran over to him, thinking he had fallen down a hole. Nothing was there. A full search of the farm found no sign of him.

legend   story based on a little bit of truth

HANGING ROCK

To the north of Melbourne, Australia, is a place of mystery. A large rock hangs above the Macedon Range of hills. The locals here talk of "the lost." A legend tells how people have climbed the rock never to return. They have vanished forever.

In 1975 Joan Lindsay wrote a book called *Picnic at Hanging Rock*. It tells of a group of schoolgirls who went for a picnic at the rock on Valentine's Day, 1900. Three girls and a teacher disappeared.

People still ask to see the newspaper report about the missing girls at the library in Melbourne. They are let down when they find out it does not exist, since the story was not true!

BENNINGTON, VERMONT: THE SITE OF MORE DISAPPEARANCES

In 1946 Paula Welden vanished on a walk. The eighteen-year-old was on the Long Trail into Glastonbury Mountain. Someone saw her go behind a rock. When other walkers reached the rock, she was nowhere to be seen. Paula has not been seen since, and no one has a clue where she went.

A scene from *Picnic at Hanging Rock*. ««

MYSTERIOUS FINDINGS

Things always disappear. There is never much mystery about it. Money, keys, pencils—we lose them all the time. They are usually just where we left them. But sometimes lost things turn up where we least expect.

MISSING RING

In 1941 a South African woman baked 150 cakes for soldiers in World War II. She sent them off to the troops, then saw that her wedding ring was missing from her finger. It just so happened that her son was one of the soldiers. He bit into a piece of cake—and there was his own mother's ring. It was soon back on her finger!

18-CARAT CARROT!

Erik Jansson from Sweden lost his gold ring in 1984. He had no idea what had happened to it. Twelve years later he dug up a carrot in his garden. The ring was around the middle of it!

Missing rings can turn up where least expected!

license legal document that gives permission to use or do something

FISHING LICENSE

Ricky Shipman lost his wallet in 1972 near Sunset Beach, North Carolina. He accidently left it in the pocket of his shorts when he was swimming, and it fell out and sunk to the ocean floor. He thought he would never find it.

Eleven years later, Ricky's driver's **license** arrived in the mail. A man had found it when he was fishing. The man had caught a large mackerel. When he cut it open, Ricky's driver's license was inside. It was in good condition since it was plastic. Ricky's name and address were clear, so he got it back. What are the chances of that happening?

Be careful what you drop into rivers—it could end up inside your next fish meal.

FISHING FOR TIME

In 1979 a Russian woman dropped her gold watch into a river. Her husband was fishing nearby and he suddenly hooked a large pike. Imagine her joy when he cut open the pike to find her watch still ticking in its stomach!

FIND OUT MORE

ORGANIZATIONS

BERMUDA TRIANGLE
Accounts and records of unexplained events in this area.
bermuda-triangle.org

AMELIA EARHART
The official website for finding out about this famous pilot.
ameliaearhart.com

BOOKS

Pflueger, Lynday. *Amelia Earhart*. Berkeley Heights, New Jersey: Enslow, 2003.

Oxlade, Chris, and Ganeri, Anita. *The Mystery of the Bermuda Triangle*. Chicago: Heinemann, 2001.

Townsend, John. *Mysteries of the Deep*. Chicago: Raintree, 2004.

WORLD WIDE WEB

If you want to find out more about disappearances, you can search the Internet using keywords such as these:

- famous + disappearances
- Bermuda Triangle

You can find your own keywords by using words or headings from this book. Use the search tips opposite to help you find the most useful websites.

SEARCH TIPS

There are billions of pages on the Internet, so it can be difficult to find exactly what you are looking for. For example, if you just type in "water" on a search engine, you will get a list of millions of web pages. These search skills will help you find useful websites more quickly:

- Know exactly what you want to find out about first.

- Use simple keywords instead of whole sentences.

- Use two to six keywords in a search, putting the most important words first.

- Be precise—only use names of people, places, or things.

- If you want to find words that go together, put quote marks around them—for example, "urban myth" or "tarantula myths."

- Use the advanced section of your search engine.

WHERE TO SEARCH

SEARCH ENGINE

A search engine looks through the entire Web and lists all the sites that match the words in the search box. It can give thousands of links, but the best matches are at the top of the list, on the first page. Try **google.com**.

SEARCH DIRECTORY

A search directory is more like a library of websites that have been sorted by a person instead of a computer. You can search by keyword or subject and browse through the different sites in the same way you would look through books on a library shelf. A good example is **yahooligans.com**.

GLOSSARY

air traffic control people and equipment that direct aircraft

anonymous from an unknown person

arrest to capture and hold someone for questioning

assassin killer who is hired to murder an important person

automatic something that works on its own

cabin room for passengers or crew on an aircraft

cargo goods carried on a ship or aircraft

challenge difficult task

curse strange power that is meant to bring harm to some people

czar emperor of Russia

database computer records for fast sorting of information

debris scattered remains

declared announced in an official way

deserted empty

destination place where a journey ends

DNA genetic code in our cells that is passed on from generation to generation. It makes us who we are.

drama tense and difficult situation

drifter someone with no real home or fixed address

equator imaginary line running east to west around the middle of the earth

fate events that a person has no control over

fibers threads that can be made into cloth

gale storm with very high winds

gorge deep, rocky ravine carved by a river

hold space in the lower part of a ship for storing the cargo

house arrest being kept prisoner in an ordinary house

identify find out someone's name

impossible cannot happen

jetty small pier or platform that juts into water for the anchoring of boats

lava hot, melted rock that comes out of volcanoes

lead piece of information that might help solve a crime

legend story based on a little bit of truth

license document that gives permission to use or do something

lifestyle way people live and spend their free time

lurk wait around, ready to strike

magnetism force that makes a ship's compass point north

maiden voyage   first journey

myth   made-up tale, told over the years and passed down

navigator   guide who plans the journey and decides which way to go

official   according to the rules and records

pressurized   sealed space in which the air pressure is controlled

rapids   fast-flowing part of a river with rocks and small waterfalls

rebel   fighter against the government

Ring of Fire   name given to the area of active volcanoes in the Pacific Ocean

rumor   story based on gossip

science fiction   made-up stories that may twist the facts of science

seabed   ocean floor; bottom of the sea

seaquake   earthquake under the ocean

ship's log   diary written up each day by the captain

sinister   harmful or evil

skipper   person in charge of a boat

SOS   signal for help. It is short for "Save Our Ship."

stalling   coming to a stop

steamship   large ship with engines driven by steam powered by burning coal

sulfur   yellow mineral used to make gunpowder, matches, etc.

summit   very top of a mountain

supernatural   forces beyond the laws of nature

surrender   give up

survive   stay alive despite dangers

tanker   huge ship for carrying liquid materials

tide   daily rise and fall of the sea

trace   sign, track, or footprint

tragic   sad and terrible, with an unhappy ending

trench   deep ditch, gully, or valley

UFO   Unidentified Flying Object

unstable   not steady, unsafe

victim   person who gets hurt or killed

violence   act that uses dangerous force

violent   angry and dangerous

volcano   opening in the surface of the earth that melted rock, hot gases, and chunks of rock ooze or explode out of

whirlpool   powerful circular current in the ocean

white-water rafting   riding down a fast-flowing river in an inflatable boat, canoe, or kayak

INDEX